THE MARKETING POCKETBOOK

By Neil Russell-Jones and Tony Fletcher

Drawings by Phil Hailstone

"A very useful introduction for anyone who wants to understand marketing terminology"
Alan Dunstan, Director - Sales and Marketing, Scottish Abbey Life

"An excellent introduction to the tools and technic
Graham Howe, Group Finance Director, Orange

D1352318

CONTENTS

INTRODUCTION

INTRODUCTION

This Pocketbook is about the fundamentals of marketing and will be useful to everyone with an interest in this field, especially:

● Those requiring an overview of the marketing process

● Those starting a marketing course, for whom it will provide a basic framework

● People interested in business in a general sense

● Non-marketers who have to input to the process

● Self-employed people

It will not make you into a marketing expert but will give you a thorough grounding in the basic concepts and theories.

For those wishing to explore topics in more detail, a further reading list is included at the end of the book.

INTRODUCTION

The book is structured into three parts:

- The introduction (chapters 1 & 2) explains the basic concepts and looks at what marketing is

- The second part (chapters 3 to 7) considers the marketing process, ie: how to go about marketing

- The final part (chapters 8 & 9) looks at putting the theory into practice

Throughout the book case studies drawn from real life are used to illustrate key points.

THE CONTEXT OF MARKETING

Running a business demands many skills:

- Financial
- People management
- Strategic thinking
- Tactical operations
- Resource usage and, of course,
- **Marketing**

None of these is more important than the other.
The best marketer will go out of business
without the proper financial controls or the
operational support to deliver to customers.

These skills can be considered in isolation
but remember, all must be present in a
business for its continued success.

MARKETING IN AN ORGANISATION

Marketing is really an ethos - a type of thinking that must **flow** throughout the company.

It is also a subset of the organisational strategy and as such assists in meeting the objectives of the organisation by ensuring that products/services are sold to the right market **at a price that will ensure profit.**

LEADERSHIP

MARKETING

OPERATIONS

SUPPORT

STRATEGY

INTRODUCTION

MARKETING FUNDAMENTAL

To succeed in business you must:

- Offer the **right product**
- To your **targeted customers**
- At a **price that is acceptable** to them
- Based on their perception of the **value**
- At a cost that allows you to be **profitable**

This is known as the **Customer Value Proposition (CVP)** and is the fundamental premise that underpins all marketing activities. We will refer to this concept throughout this Pocketbook.

Successful companies understand their CVPs and use them to guide their thinking.

INTRODUCTION

CVP DEFINED

A CVP expresses what an organisation (or part of an organisation) is all about.
It should:

- Define customer needs that the firm is trying to meet
- Identify at whom it is targeting its activities
- State why the firm is different from the competition
- Explain the benefit of this difference to customers
- Indicate how the firm will provide its offerings

A CVP serves as a framework within which to orient your business.

CVP EXAMPLES

To illustrate the concept of Customer Value Propositions (CVPs), here are some examples:

For a corner shop it might be: To provide a small selection of consumer goods, in a convenient location with convenient opening times and friendly local service, therefore allowing a slightly higher price to be charged.

For a retail bank: To provide a place for customers to deposit securely, and subsequently disburse conveniently, their funds.

For a fast food outlet: To provide value for money food and drinks of consistent quality globally, served quickly in a friendly manner, to younger people and families.

A large organisation would have more than one CVP, depending on its customers, eg: a large bank would probably have one for retail, corporate, financial institutions, offshore clientele, etc. A utility company would need to address both domestic and corporate customers.

Try to create a CVP for your own organisation.

WHAT IS MARKETING?

DEFINITIONS

There are many definitions of marketing. Here are a few:

- **"The aim of marketing is to make selling superfluous"** - Peter Drucker
  (ie: you must understand the customer so well that the product/service sells itself)

- **"A combination of selling, advertising and PR"** - the widely held view of the public

- **"The performance of business activities that direct the flow of goods and services from producer to consumer or user"** - American Marketing Association

- **"Getting the right goods, to the right people, in the right place, at the right time, at the right price, with the right level of communication profitably"** - Chartered Institute of Marketing (UK)

- **"Consumption is the sole end and purpose of all production"** - Adam Smith, Wealth of Nations (ie: only produce what someone will buy)

In fact, they all mean the same thing, ie: find out what customers want and produce/deliver it.

SELLING VS MARKETING

Selling

- 'Introverted'
- Inward looking
- Starts with the product
- Shorter time horizon
- Is about revenue this week
- Focused on one aspect of your service

Marketing

- 'Extroverted'
- Outward looking
- Starts with the customer
- Longer time horizon
- About profit this year
- The ethos of the organisation

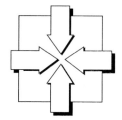 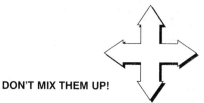

DON'T MIX THEM UP!

WHAT IS MARKETING?

TERMINOLOGY

Throughout the book we refer to products, services and brands. By these we mean:

Product   A tangible item, such as a hammer, a car, a shirt, breakfast cereal, etc

Service   The provision of something that is intangible, such as an air flight, advice, a night in an hotel, an evening at the theatre

('Product' is used to refer to both products and services.)

Brand   These are the names under which products and services are offered. They can be umbrella brands - under which a group of products/services are offered (eg: Cadbury's, Mars, McDonalds) - or they can be specific (eg: *Dairy Milk* - Cadbury's; *Snickers* - Mars; *Big Mac* - McDonalds)

Brands have significant value, can be bought and sold, and must be nourished and protected.

BEING CUSTOMER FOCUSED

Marketing is all about giving the customer what he wants.

This encapsulates:

- **Product**   The properties of your service
- **Price**   The right price and value
- **Place**   Availability
- **Promotion**   Informing customers in a manner that they understand

Marketing people call this the **4 Ps** (more later), **but** it is driven by the **Customer Value Proposition (CVP).**

WHAT IS MARKETING?

4 KEY ELEMENTS

The four key elements of
marketing are, in order:

- **Research** - finding out
- **Strategy** - the vision
- **Planning** - the 'how'
- **Tactics** - at the sharp end

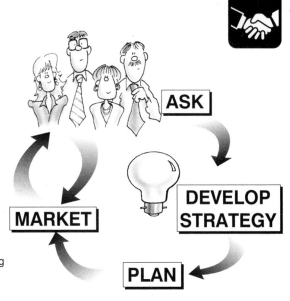

These will be addressed during
the rest of the book.

TARGETING YOUR 'BUYER'

It is important to understand who
the ultimate buyer is (as per the CVP).
The supply chain can be long
and complex, so you also
need to identify each of the
buyers in the chain. Often
a producer does not or
cannot go to the end buyer.

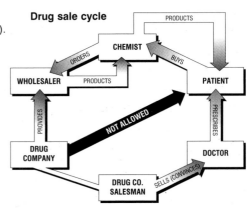

Drug sale cycle

HOLISTIC APPROACH

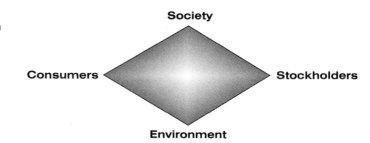

Marketing can be viewed from many perspectives; some organisations look at only one, others at many.

Some organisations follow a holistic approach (eg: McDonalds, Co-op Bank, John Lewis) with great success. The approach tries to satisfy the expectations of all four competing, and at times conflicting, aspects. It may be more expensive and much more complicated to manage these conflicting demands, but it may also pay dividends in the long run.

WHAT IS MARKETING?

HOLISTIC APPROACH

MCDONALDS

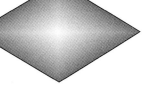

Society
Community involvement
Charity support
Family orientation

Consumers
Quality
Value
Service
Cleanliness
Nutrition information
Consistency

Stockholders
Turnover $9.8 billion
Profit $1.4 billion
Franchise operations
Investment
(McDonald's University)

Environment
Recyclable packaging
Products from sustainable sources

RESEARCHING YOUR CUSTOMERS

WHAT IS MARKET RESEARCH?

The systematic collection of information on existing or potential markets, for analysis and subsequent action.

In order to be successful at marketing (ie: to get the CVP right) you need to find out what is going on in your chosen market, specifically:

- Identify customers **needs** and **wants**
- Understand the **competition**
- Analyse the **market dynamics**

Then use this information to provide a 'package':

- To meet those needs
- That is better than the competition
- Which is within the market parameters

NEEDS AND WANTS

'Needs' and 'wants' are very different. It is critical to understand the difference:

- **Needs** are real

- **Wants** are aspirational

Research must find out **needs** not **wants**, eg:

'I **want** a Mont Blanc pen. However, maybe I only really **need** a biro or a pencil? Or just something to write with? Or perhaps only some method of communication? Or maybe a fashion accessory? Or is it a statement of wealth I'm looking for (conspicuous consumption)?'

Advertising, however, can often appeal to **wants** - eg: those linking glamorous lifestyles to products (eg: *Martini*) or sex (eg: *Obsession*).

WHY RESEARCH?

- As an input to analysis and subsequent decision-making
- To find new markets
- To ascertain your customers' real needs
- To find out what your competition is doing, or why you are not doing well
- To establish the **Customer Value Proposition**
- Research helps to:
  - minimise risk
  - focus efforts
  - maximise return

It is important to know what you want to find out before you start, so as not to waste time, effort and cost.

RESEARCHING YOUR CUSTOMERS

HOW TO RESEARCH

Before starting, clarify your objectives:

- Why you want the information
- What you will do with it
- The format it should be in

There are many ways of getting information but first ask, 'Has it already been done by somebody else?' (much cheaper and easier).

You find this out by carrying out **desk research.**

If not, then you have to go to the source - **field research.**

DESK RESEARCH

This is surprisingly productive and there is a plethora of sources, including books, periodicals, newspapers, directories and electronically stored data (CD, on-line, Internet). A brief list would include:

- Trade Associations (very relevant sector information)
- Market research firms (eg: Gallup, AGB, Nielsen, MORI, MINTEL)
- Government publications (HMSO)
- Commercial publishers (Keynote is one of the largest)
- Company information providers (Dun & Bradstreet, Extel, Who owns Whom)
- Trade journals (excellent surveys, as well as commentary on trends)
- Press (daily reading and searches)

Tips:
- Visit your local/specialised library (London Business School, Manchester Business School, etc)
- If you need help, ask the Market Research Society for a list of members
- Keep a detailed file of information with a précis on top
- Be careful to distinguish between facts and opinion

FIELD RESEARCH

If you cannot find the information you want by desk research, then you have to find out for yourself (or employ a specialist). To maximise the benefit, plan properly.
Key steps will be:

Objective	What do you need to know?	
Samples	From whom?	
Method	What process will you use?	
Structure	What type of questions?	
Analysis	What will you do with the information?	
Cost	How much will you pay and is it worth it?	
Timing	When do you need it?	

RESEARCHING YOUR CUSTOMERS

OBJECTIVES

Normally, the objective of market research is to find out **in detail** what your target customers want.

You must ask questions in such a way that the answers provide direct input into your strategy, eg:

- Shall we make it bigger or smaller?
- Is the size okay?
- What colours should we use?
- Do you want faster delivery at a higher price?

THE SAMPLES - HOW LARGE?

The number of people questioned is very relevant to research as, logically, the larger the sample the more accurate the results should be. The more questioned, however, the higher the cost.

Fortunately, it is not necessary to ask everyone in your target market segment, because a lot of work has already been carried out in this area (statistics). Moreover, there is considerable agreement on the actual size of sample necessary to represent the 'population'. These numbers are surprisingly low because, after a certain point, there is little appreciable improvement in accuracy.

This is known as the **'statistically significant number'** and for consumer goods it is in the low hundreds (out of a potential market of millions!).

SAMPLE SEGMENTATION

For research to be meaningful, you must be able to rely on the robustness of the results. It must, therefore, be conducted with the same type of people (**an homogeneous range**) who display similar characteristics and who would respond in the same manner to the same questions. This is known as **Segmentation** and could include:

- Age (tots, teens, twenties, middle, old, etc)
- Sex
- Residential neighbourhood (ACORN, postcodes)
- Education levels (O levels/GCSEs, A levels, degree [science, arts])
- Lifestyle (hobbies)
- Lifecycles (single, married, children, retired)
- Occupation (blue, grey, white collar)
- Socio-economic groups (AB, C1, C2, DE)
- Religion   • Culture   • Regional

They can be used singly or in combination. Segmentation is at the heart of the CVP and therefore successful marketing.

TYPES OF QUESTIONS

There are two types of questions - **Quantitative** and **Qualitative.**

Quantitative questions require a specific answer, eg:

- How many (number) ...?
- Do you like (yes/no) ...?
- How do you rate (1 to 5) ...?

The answers are easier to analyse because they will always fit the pattern.
However, they may be inaccurate since they do not allow for 'maybe's' and 'if's'.

TYPES OF QUESTIONS

Qualitative questions allow people to describe feelings. They are, therefore, much harder to analyse, although probably more accurate and revealing. Examples:

● How could we improve our service?
● Which new feature would you like to see?
● How could you have enjoyed the flight more?

Many people find it easier to express themselves orally rather than give written responses. To obtain useful answers you must use questions that are unambiguous, precise, clear and will yield analysable answers. Many questionnaires fail this simple test, thus rendering the information collected useless or meaningless.

The order is important as a prior question can influence a following answer. Example: Do you like Bloggs beer? Which is your favourite beer? The answer to the second question is likely to be influenced by the brand name appearing in the first question.

ANALYSIS: MEASURING THE ANSWERS

Your inputs (answers to the questions) must be output (analysis) driven.

Therefore, structure the questions in order to give the answers that, after analysis, will give you the data you need.

Think about how to analyse the answers (if you have 10,000 responses you are going to need a computer to carry out the analysis). Creating a database will also help, as this will allow correlating analysis to be carried out.

Consider these issues:
- Is one answer dependent on another?
- What if some answers are missing/unclear?
- How will you categorise subjective opinions
  (is 'OK' the same as 'average' or 'acceptable')?
- People are often inconsistent in filling out boxes
  (using a cross sometimes means 'yes', at other times it can mean 'no').
- How will you present the data and the conclusions drawn?
- Information is expensive to collect and analyse; therefore, collect only
  what you need.

RESEARCHING YOUR CUSTOMERS

TIMING

To maximise the use of your research, you must ensure that it is delivered when you want it. Set deadlines by working backwards from when you need it.

Use a bar chart or Gantt chart (see next page) to give you a visual picture of the timings.

Typical stages are:

- Scoping to set the framework
- Set-up phase (hiring contractors, preparing questionnaires, samples, purchasing mailing lists)
- Desk research
- Test research (piloting) where you check the approach and questions
- Full research (there may be more than one phase)
- Analysis (leave plenty of time for this as further research may be needed)
- Reporting

TIMING

Activity

Scoping	
Set-up phase	
Desk research	
Test research	
Full research	
Analysis	
Reporting	

TIME

RESEARCHING YOUR CUSTOMERS

COST

The cost can vary widely from a few hundred pounds to the millions spent by multi-nationals on major consumer brands.

It is relatively easy to assess the costs with this simple procedure:

● Scope out the activities that you think you will need (eg: 100 telephone calls, 20 face-to-face interviews, etc)

● Assess the amount of time that this requires

● Identify the daily cost of your own staff or external staff (of the right calibre)

● Add in the time for questionnaire preparation, analysis and report writing

● Compare this cost with external quotes

MARKET RESEARCH - METHODS

THE METHODS

Several methods are available.

The main ones are:

- Telephone interviews
- Written questionnaires
- Street interviews
- Face-to-face interviews

Others you may come across are:

- Product testing
- Consumer panels
- Observation
- Focus groups

You must choose the right combination of methods that will yield the answers you need. Each has pros and cons as shown on the following pages.

Never mix up research and selling! This is called 'sugging' and really upsets people.

MARKET RESEARCH - METHODS

TELEPHONE INTERVIEWS

Using the telephone to get information from people - simple in concept; difficult in execution.

- Relatively inexpensive
- Can be focused
- Quick
- People prefer talking to writing

But:
- People are suspicious of such calls
- Spurious responses may be given
- Timing (when to call) is critical

Tips:
- Have a structured script
- Give relevant information that won't prejudice answers
- Tell them how long it will take
- If talking to business, make a note of whom you interviewed

MARKET RESEARCH - METHODS

WRITTEN QUESTIONNAIRES

Use is very widespread, eg: hotels, airlines, publishers, postal questionnaires, membership surveys.

- A passive research method that relies on goodwill
- Easy and cheap
- Better quality information than from oral interviews (time to think or research)
- Structure is vital - simple, clear and not subjective (multiple choice is easier to analyse than unstructured responses)

Tips:
- To get required response, multiply the number by 20 (5% is average rate of return)
- A letter addressed 'Dear Mr Smith' is more likely to evoke a response than one starting 'Dear Sir/Madam/Miss/Ms'
- Pre-paid envelopes can increase response dramatically
- Small gifts are often given as a reward for participation
- Linking questionnaires with guarantee forms will get a good response
- Questions should be simple, unambiguous and specific
- Send out a trial sample first to check results

WRITTEN QUESTIONNAIRES

EXAMPLES

Type	Description	Example
Likert	Shows agreement levels	*Small shops give better service than larger ones:* ☐ strongly disagree ☒ disagree ☐ neutral ☐ agree ☐ strongly agree
Bipolar	A scale between two bipolar words on which respondent places a mark to represent level of feelings	*This restaurant is:* clean _ _ X_ _ _ _ _ _ _ _ _ _ _ _ _ dirty friendly _ _ _ _ _ _ _ _ _ _ X_ _ _ _ _ unfriendly warm _ _ _ _ _ _ _ _ X_ _ _ _ _ _ _ cold
Importance	Rates the weighting of a factor	*Service to me is:* ☐ critical ☐ important ☒ neutral ☐ minor ☐ unimportant
Buying propensity	Measures the likelihood of buying	*If cable was available would you:* ☐ definitely buy ☐ probably buy ☒ might buy ☐ probably not buy ☐ definitely not buy
Rating	Measures an attribute from 'poor' to 'excellent'	*The food in your staff canteen is:* 1. poor 2. fair 3. ok ☒ 4. very good 5. excellent
Multiple choice	Offers three or more choices	*What type of book did you buy?* ☐ horror ☐ western ☐ romance ☐ detective ☐ biography ☐ cookery ☐ sport ☒ educational ☐ other
Binary	Gives a choice between two answers	*Are you a member of a book club?* ☒ Yes ☐ No

STREET INTERVIEWS

Involves researchers stopping people in the street. Initially, interviewees are asked a few personal questions, to check they meet criteria, and then specifics.

Technique similar to telephone interviews, except that visual aids can be used, eg: 'Which design do you prefer?' - shows several; 'Which taste do you prefer?' - offers several drinks.

Tips:
- Segments must be wide enough to be practical
- Questions should be short; remember, you're stopping people in the street
- Locations will be critical as you will get a different mix at different sites
- More locations, more expense
- Get professional help (better experienced at getting the right responses without alienating prospects)
- If you do it yourself, use the following self-help guide

STREET INTERVIEWS

SELF-HELP GUIDE

- Prepare questions in advance
- Test them on a small sample
- Stand in good light
- Avoid a threatening appearance
- Smile all the time
- Carry some ID
- Prepare for weather
- Accept 'No' gracefully
- Survey sites in advance
- If relevant, get permission (eg: you may need a stand/table for visuals)
- Maximum time should be 15 minutes or less
- If possible, give a small reward
- Thank them for their time

FACE-TO-FACE INTERVIEWS

A structured conversation, guided to ensure the correct ground is covered.

Confirm the meeting in writing beforehand and, if relevant, give some idea of the nature of the discussion and probable timing. The interviewer should have sent an agenda (for business-to-business) prior to the meeting.

Usually the client name is not disclosed, to avoid possible prejudice in answers.

Tips:
- Arrive in good time
- Keep to agreed timing
- Tick off items on agenda
- Guide conversation but don't ask leading questions
- Thank interviewee
- If relevant, agree to send interviewee the results or an abstract
- If it is not working, leave politely

PRODUCT TESTS

Frequently used in consumer markets (eg: to test confectionery, drinks, household products, etc) but also in other industries (eg: software).

Product is sent to several consumers, who report back on their feelings, etc. Also common to establish sites, to test and get instant feedback (known as 'Hall test').

Tips:
- Choose an appropriate site (village hall, pedestrian precinct, shop/factory site)
- Ensure all participants either fill in a questionnaire or are de-briefed
- If using multiple sites, ensure same structure is followed
- Make sure site is representative (don't test a new beer outside a brewery or a Temperance hall)
- Have enough staff to capture spontaneous remarks/reactions

CONSUMER PANELS

Also called Omnibus surveys. Panel members fill in a diary of their purchases over an agreed period of time (ie: they are a permanent sample of the market). Used only for Fast Moving Consumer Goods (FMCG) due to the buying cycles.

There is a question mark over whether responses are natural or not; the type of people who agree to be on the panel may not be truly representative.

Tips:
- Use a specialist firm

OBSERVATION

Often used for FMCG to note consumer behaviour in, for example, shops or centres. Has some key advantages: is totally objective (no questions/answers) and records only current behaviour (untainted by past history or future intentions). However, it is time consuming and expensive and will only yield limited results.

Tips:
- Make sure it will give you the right information before using it
- Customers should be unaware of the observation which should be discreet

FOCUS GROUPS

Involves bringing together six to twelve people, to discuss specific issues. Similar to face-to-face interviews except that it brings in group dynamics.

Participants are put into a relaxing environment, either a comfortable room or a private dining room (meal provided). The facilitator guides the discussion and the conversation is minuted.

Often used for industry trend analysis, strategy discussions and product comparisons. Also common to use them to kick start a research campaign by ensuring all issues/angles have been considered.

Tips:
- Needs facilitating - a free lunch is not a focus group!
- Specialist facilitator will ensure better results
- Pick members carefully to get optimum blend of experience and skills
- Make sure all group members express opinions

PUTTING IT TOGETHER

Consolidate the data gathered into a market research report.
Typically, this will include the following sections:

- Market size
- Market dynamics (growing, shrinking)
- Competitors
- Customers' needs
- Your current position

This enables you to
develop your strategy.

DEVELOPING A MARKETING STRATEGY

DEVELOPING A MARKETING STRATEGY

OVERVIEW

A strategy is a holistic view of the organisation's purpose.
It is usually expressed in terms of:

- Long-term objectives
- Actions to achieve these
- Resource allocations
  necessary to support
  them

A strategy usually supports an over-arching 'vision' of the future, linked to a mission statement. Beneath it will be detailed plans and tactics.

DEVELOPING A MARKETING STRATEGY

THE VISION

The vision is usually couched in very high-level terms, eg:

- **Coca Cola** wanted every GI to be able to buy its product anywhere in the world

- **Wedgwood** wanted to sell crockery to every worker

- **Henry Ford** had a vision of everybody driving one of his cars

The mission statement elaborates on this.

DEVELOPING A MARKETING STRATEGY

MISSION

The mission (a US term that has virtually been adopted worldwide) is a statement of what the organisation's objectives are. It might be:

- 'To be the leading retail bank in the UK, as measured by market share, capital strength and profitability'.

It will then go on to state the high-level 'hows':

- 'We will achieve this by increasing our telephone banking service and by reducing our branch network by: concentrating only on profitable customers; offering a personalised service; and offering 24-hour banking; etc'

And then state the implication of this:

- 'We will have excellent IT support; adequate training for staff; remuneration linked to performance; etc.'

It is within this framework that strategies and policies are set.

A mission must be:
- Market focused
- Based on core strengths/ competencies
- Motivating

MARKETING FRAMEWORK

A marketing strategy can be set at organisational level, business unit level or lower down. Wherever it is set, the strategy always comprises a co-ordinated set of decisions that establish a framework for marketing. Included are:

- Target markets

- Marketing mix (4 Ps)

- Expenditure

- Positioning of products/services
  (price vs quality - 'pile it high, sell it cheap' vs Rolls-Royce)

Marketing is expensive and it pays to concentrate your efforts. The strategy will, therefore, focus on those segments identified as likely to respond best to the chosen CVP(s).

DEVELOPING A MARKETING STRATEGY

STEPS TO SETTING-UP

The diagram opposite shows the steps to be followed in setting-up your marketing strategy.

1a Analyse your company (SWOT)
1b Analyse the markets (segmentation)
1c Establish marketing policy (general rules)
2   Conduct gap analysis (What is missing/poor?)
3a Develop products/services where appropriate
3b Formulate the strategy
4   Undertake planning
5   Implement it

DEVELOPING A MARKETING STRATEGY

STEPS TO SETTING-UP

ROUTE MAP

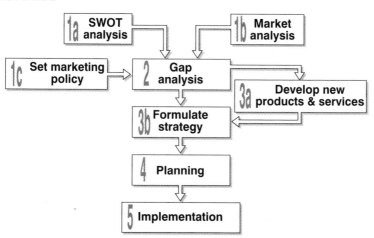

SWOT analysis — 1a

Market analysis — 1b

Set marketing policy — 1c

Gap analysis — 2

Develop new products & services — 3a

Formulate strategy — 3b

Planning — 4

Implementation — 5

DEVELOPING A MARKETING STRATEGY

1a SWOT ANALYSIS

This term stands for analysis of:

Strengths
Weaknesses
Opportunities, and
Threats

This is the pre-strategic analysis that must be undertaken. The information yielded allows the strategy to address the issues uncovered (playing to strengths, correcting weaknesses, attacking opportunities and defending threats).

Whilst developed for a general organisational strategy, it applies equally well to the marketing strategy.

You might find it useful to think in terms of a strategy representing the overview of how to get to where you want to be (the vision).

DEVELOPING A MARKETING STRATEGY

1b MARKET ANALYSIS

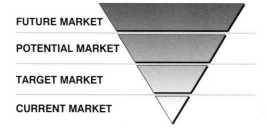

FUTURE MARKET

POTENTIAL MARKET

TARGET MARKET

CURRENT MARKET

In analysing the market, consider:

- The market you currently serve and what you can do here
- The market you will be targeting and the implications
- The potential market, of which your segment is but a part
- The future market, ie: taking a longer-time horizon

DEVELOPING A MARKETING STRATEGY

1b MARKET ANALYSIS

SEGMENTATION

It is impossible to be all things to all people. Therefore, study your proposed markets and focus on the key parts - the segments - and direct best efforts there.

Segments are defined as: 'sets of buyers who have similar needs and respond to marketing offers in similar ways'.

Segments differ depending on the business. A restaurant, for example, might have the following segments:

- Lunchtime trade
- Pre-theatre parties
- Late night diners
- 'Families'
- Weekend meal/special occasion customers

Each will have different needs and will require different marketing (price, promotion, menu).

1b MARKET ANALYSIS

SEGMENTATION

Life is complex. Consequently, many buyers fall into several segments, eg: cars are purchased for utility, price, style, speed, 'coolness', marque, origin, features (boot size, soft top), etc; and buyers can be categorised into socio-economic groups, nationality, residential neighbourhoods, age, etc. This makes it very difficult to focus.

Some producers focus on one segment (eg: Aston Martin targets the very rich) whilst others serve several (eg: Ford, General Motors, VW).

The key is how an organisation views itself - as a **car** manufacturer (Aston Martin) or as **vehicle** manufacturers producing cars, vans, lorries, tractors, etc (Ford, GM). This view changes the market and requires a more complicated strategy or, rather, set of strategies.

DEVELOPING A MARKETING STRATEGY

1b MARKET ANALYSIS

SEGMENTATION STEPS

- Decide upon what bases you will segment
- Analyse the resulting segments and produce a précis of them
- Analyse the attractiveness of those segments to you (based on SWOT analysis)
- Prioritise them, and select the top ones
- Decide which products you will offer to each
- Choose the position of the offering(s)
- Develop a micro-marketing plan for each, ie: the CVPs

Coutts & Co, a subsidiary of UK bank NatWest, targets one specific segment known as High Net Worth Individuals (HINWIS). It feels that these customers have different needs and will pay for specialist service to meet those needs. Accordingly, it offers a very personal service, including funds management, from frock-coated bankers, and charges higher fees than high street banks.

DEVELOPING A MARKETING STRATEGY

1c MARKETING POLICY

Policy can be thought of as a set of general rules that govern the day-to-day execution of strategies and tactics. It is set usually at the highest level in an organisation and will normally consider intangible concepts such as customer service (eg: Marks & Spencer, where anyone arguing with a customer is likely to be disciplined; or John Lewis, where they are 'never knowingly undersold').

This policy will cut across strategies and tactics, and affect how you carry out your operations. It is intended to establish the broad framework of how an organisation wishes to be positioned in the market - notwithstanding any short-term price/quality differences such as sales or undersells.

It supports the image that the company wants to convey in the marketplace. It would be surprising if goods bought at any of the quality stores were of shoddy quality (or if they were, that they would not be exchanged/refunded immediately). Similarly, you would expect companies such as Yves St Laurent or Hermes to resist vigorously demands for vast discounts which would undermine their cachet.

DEVELOPING A MARKETING STRATEGY

1c MARKETING POLICY

THE QUALITY/PRICE TRADE-OFF

QUALITY vs PRICE

PRICE

Dreams not perfume

Pile it high
Sell it cheap

QUALITY

In formulating your policy, decide where on these axes you will place the offering.
Each point on the grid represents a trade-off between price and quality. It is very difficult
to enforce a high price if quality is low. Similarly, high quality implies high costs which
must be recouped via high prices.

Compare the quality of, for example, a bath-sheet bought in a departmental store for, say,
£30 and one for sale on a market stall at, say, £12. Both purchases involve a price/quality
trade-off and both vendors are positioning themselves in a different part of the grid.

DEVELOPING A MARKETING STRATEGY

2 GAP ANALYSIS

This involves taking the internal analysis and comparing it with the external analysis (from your research) to see how your company measures up and what is missing if you are to meet your objectives.

Once this gap analysis has been carried out, you then need to take steps to close the gap. Selective benchmarking can often be of use here.

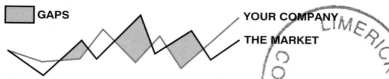

You only close the gaps where the action required will deliver substantial dividends, where it is cost-effective or where it is a fundamental issue.

The objective is to make your products acceptable in your target segments and, ideally, to make them more effective than your competitors'. For example, there has recently been an increase in the number of car manufacturers offering off-road vehicles and people carriers', reflecting the growing demand for these products.

DEVELOPING A MARKETING STRATEGY

3a DEVELOPING NEW PRODUCTS/SERVICES

Your research/analysis might indicate that there are gaps between what you are offering and either what your competitors are offering or what your customers need - or both. In this event, you need to develop new products, or improve your existing ones, to fill the gaps. This can take time depending on the nature of your business and must be factored into your planning and timing.

Where products have a long lead time (eg: pharmaceuticals, aerospace industry) then you will need to develop an interim strategy until your new products are ready, and a further strategy to capitalise on these.

3a DEVELOPING NEW PRODUCTS/SERVICES

TYPICAL PRODUCT LIFE CYCLE

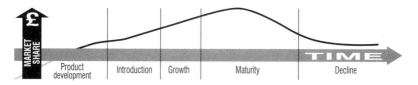

Most products follow this cycle and it can be used in planning your marketing. You need different tactics at each stage to address the issues.

- Customers need to be told about a new product as they won't have heard of it
- As the market expands during growth, so too does the need for market support
- Following growth, you must fight hard to retain market share
- Finally, during decline, you exit or re-launch with a new product (eg: soap powders)

Different products have different cycles. A fashion item (stack-heeled shoes) might only last months, whereas others, say cars or food, can last much longer (eg: the VW Golf which has been around for years with some variations, or Heinz baked beans which have hardly varied at all).

(63)

3a DEVELOPING NEW PRODUCTS/SERVICES

RISK / REWARD TRADE-OFF

In establishing your strategy, it is necessary to consider the risk/reward trade-off. The matrix on the facing page analyses four possible strategies and the consequent risk/return from their implementation.

Company A has three strategies:

❶ To launch a brand new product in its home market

❷ To expand its current number one bestseller into a new market

❸ To introduce a new product into a new market

By plotting these on the matrix, you can see that:

● Product development = higher risk

● Market development = medium risk

● Diversification = very risky

A much less risky strategy is to sell more of your goods in your current markets - known as penetration (gaining market share).

The potential cost of each and the likely return must be analysed to ensure that the benefits are realisable and quantifiable before entering into the plan.

DEVELOPING A MARKETING STRATEGY

3a DEVELOPING NEW PRODUCTS/SERVICES

PRODUCT/MARKET EXPANSION GRID (Ansoff matrix)

	EXISTING PRODUCTS	NEW PRODUCTS
EXISTING MARKETS	1 MARKET PENETRATION *LOW RISK*	2 PRODUCT DEVELOPMENT *HIGHER RISK* ❶
NEW MARKETS	3 MARKET DEVELOPMENT *MEDIUM RISK* ❷	4 DIVERSIFICATION *HIGHEST RISK* ❸

Type of Action	**Where the company is looking to increase sales by:**
1 MARKET PENETRATION	Increasing current product/service sales in current markets by better marketing
2 PRODUCT DEVELOPMENT	Developing new products/services for its current markets
3 MARKET DEVELOPMENT	Taking its current products/services to new markets
4 DIVERSIFICATION	Developing new products/services for new markets

DEVELOPING A MARKETING STRATEGY

4 PLANNING

Having set your policy and, within this framework, decided on your strategy (which may or may not require new product development) you need to plan how you are going to implement your strategy. The **How** rather than the **What**.

This requires an understanding of the marketing mix (the 4 Ps) and a written and agreed plan. Read on to find out more.

UNDERSTANDING
THE MARKETING MIX

UNDERSTANDING THE MARKETING MIX

THE 4 Ps

This is a key concept - the actions that a company uses to develop its business.

It is often represented, from the marketer's point of view, as encompassing four prime elements:

1 **P**roduct (or Service)
2 **P**rice
3 **P**lace
4 **P**romotion

The four **P**s.

The blend of these four elements shapes the way a product is marketed.
**Get this right and you will be in marketing heaven;
get it wrong and hell will beckon.**

UNDERSTANDING THE MARKETING MIX

THE CHALLENGE

The challenge of the marketing mix is to get the balance right. All firms have finite resources (human/financial) and they need to be allocated effectively.

While research will help you here, there is no right way to allocate resources. Instead, you go through an interactive process, starting with the theoretical marketing mix which is progressively refined in response to feedback from the marketing. This will help you achieve your goals.

BLENDING THE MIX

MARKETING MIX

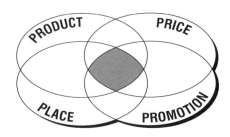

The blend differs from product to product, from location to location and from business to business but they need to be integrated to support the CVP.

Each of the four Ps is discussed in turn.

UNDERSTANDING THE MARKETING MIX

1. PRODUCT

Issues to consider include:

- Customer benefits
- Quality
- Design
- Technical features
- Branding
- Packaging
- Service
- Training

UNDERSTANDING THE MARKETING MIX

2. PRICE

There is much more to pricing than choosing a number. Your price may be used by consumers as a measure of all the benefits you offer. Then they decide if you offer good value or not (remember the CVP). It is the most flexible of the four, and you can use short-term or long-term pricing to maximise opportunities.

Some things that you can do with pricing:

- Discounts
- Bundling items or pricing separately
- Lump sum or piece rate
- Rebates or loyalty schemes
- Undersell the competition

3. PLACE

This is about getting your product in front of your customers.

There are many methods of doing this - known as **distribution channels** or **supply chains**.

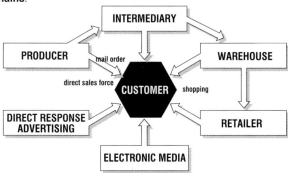

UNDERSTANDING THE MARKETING MIX

3. PLACE

DISTRIBUTION CHANNELS

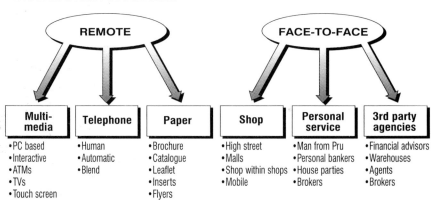

REMOTE			FACE-TO-FACE		
Multi-media	**Telephone**	**Paper**	**Shop**	**Personal service**	**3rd party agencies**
•PC based	•Human	•Brochure	•High street	•Man from Pru	•Financial advisors
•Interactive	•Automatic	•Catalogue	•Malls	•Personal bankers	•Warehouses
•ATMs	•Blend	•Leaflet	•Shop within shops	•House parties	•Agents
•TVs		•Inserts	•Mobile	•Brokers	•Brokers
•Touch screen		•Flyers			

Channels can be both remote and face-to-face. Each has pros and cons.

4. PROMOTION

It is vital to tell your customers about your products or they will not know where to go to get them.

Some of the more common methods include:

- Advertising (TV, papers, posters, radio, cinema, videos)
- Direct Mail
- Telephone selling
- Brochures and catalogues
- Exhibitions, 3rd party endorsements
- Sponsoring events, items
- Sales force

The cost varies from method to method.
Ensure that the blend you select is
cost effective for **you**.

UNDERSTANDING THE MARKETING MIX

MARKETING MIX IN PRACTICE

Manufacturers take account of their:

- Segments
- Resources - financial/human
- Market characteristics
- CVP

Then they construct a communications plan (part of the marketing plan) based on the 4 Ps. Example:

Price   :   will set our price at £3.95 (competition sell at £4.15)
Product   :   will add a bell and whistle
Place   :   will sell through garages as well as our usual retailers
Promotion :   will use direct mail (30%); TV ads (40%); in store (30%)

Different companies use different combinations.

MARKETING MIX IN PRACTICE

EXAMPLES

The marketing mix must be a blend of the four elements but here are some examples where one predominates:

- **Tie Rack**, a great success story, decided in the 1980s that the key element would be **place** - outlets were mostly located in stations where people could quickly buy from a wide range of good quality ties

- **Tesco** for a long time sold on **price**, but has gradually changed to selling on product quality using major promotional campaigns; Kwik-Save sells on **price** in the same market

- **Marks & Spencer** sells on **product** and only its own brands; perfume and luxury goods are similarly product oriented (exclusivity)

- **Soap products** tend to be sold on **promotion**, ie: through heavy advertising (as are many beers)

Of course, other elements of the marketing mix are employed here, but the examples given demonstrate a preference for a particular element.

CUSTOMERS' PERSPECTIVE - THE 4 Cs

From the customers' point of view, the 4 Ps can be seen to represent four benefits - often called **the 4 Cs**:

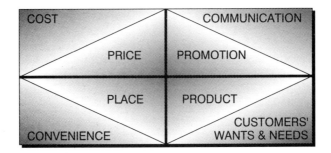

This is a very good way of testing the CVP: does it meet the 4Cs?

UNDERSTANDING THE MARKETING MIX

THE 4 Cs - COST

Perceived cost to the customer:

- May be more than just financial
- Must reflect value:
  - more for more **(upper end of scale)**
  - less for less **(pile it high - sell it cheap)**
  - more for less **(bargain)**

  (NB: **less for more** is usually unsuccessful!)

You must, therefore, get the cost right to equalise the cost/benefit equation of the CVP.

THE 4 Cs - CONVENIENCE

You have to make it as easy as possible for your customers to obtain your product. What seems fine to you may not to them. People are essentially lazy and most will trade convenience for much else.

Some good examples where convenience has driven change:

- The rise of direct banking over the phone, 24 hours a day

- The change from local shopping to once-a-week visits to out-of-town megastores selling most things

- Mail order catalogues and freephone telephone order lines

- Home visits by representatives to collect orders

- Greater use of 'plastic' (Switch, MasterCard, Visa and in-house cards, regional cards, Mondex)

UNDERSTANDING THE MARKETING MIX

THE 4 Cs - COMMUNICATION

Every day customers receive hundreds of messages telling them to buy.
Make sure that:

- Your message stands out from the general clutter

- You tell customers about your offering in their terms **not** yours

- You focus on **benefits** not technical features

- Your communication is **targeted** appropriately (do not advertise meat in a vegetarian weekly)

THE 4 Cs - CUSTOMER NEEDS & WANTS

Needs differ:

- Across time (eg: as consumers get more sophisticated or as they age - lifecycle)

- According to circumstance (segment your customer groups)

- As the 'price-benefit' equation changes

- As fashion shifts (washing machines and vacuum cleaners, originally a luxury, are now considered essential)

Understand customer needs through research and anticipate the changes in your offerings.

A GRAPHIC VIEW

Different pricing mixes can be viewed graphically to demonstrate the variations in tactics. The two examples below are competing on **Price/Product** A and **Promotion/Place** B, but both need to have a mix of all four components, reflecting their respective CVPs.

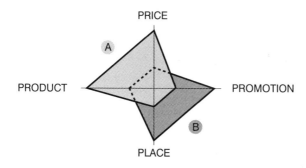

FINAL THOUGHTS ON MIX

- Make sure that there is the right balance between the four elements to reflect your CVP

- Think in terms of the four Cs rather than four Ps initially, then convert so that you reflect the customer's perception

- Change the mix to reflect different segments

- Be flexible and vary to suit needs

- Make sure that the sums add up before you spend a lot on promotion or cut prices

MARKETING PLANNING

SUMMARY

OBJE...

MARKET

COMPETITION

MARKETING PLANNING

PLAN OVERVIEW

A written plan is vital to focus your marketing effort and to control it.

What is a marketing plan?

- Statement of intent
- Attempt at quantifying the future
- Cohesive structure
- Signposts for action
- Base for evaluation and feedback
- Outcome of a logical process

What does planning involve?

- Management and executive time/input
- Commitment
- Cost
- Research
- Assumptions
- Review

It is important to get it right (or at least less wrong than the opposition).

MARKETING PLANNING

WHAT THE PLAN CONTAINS

The plan is the framework for putting into action the marketing strategy.
It should contain:

1	Summary	7	Selling plan
2	Marketing objectives	8	Communication plan
3	Market characteristics	9	Timetable
4	Competition overview	10	Responsibilities
5	Product position	11	Budgets
6	Distribution mechanisms	12	Appendices

MARKETING PLANNING

WHAT THE PLAN CONTAINS

1. Summary
The summary is a stand-alone overview which will give readers a good idea of the contents of the plan, enabling them to investigate areas more fully within the main body of text.

2. Marketing objectives
A statement of the objectives that the plan is attempting to achieve.
A plan will be needed for each business unit, product or brand, depending on how you divide your organisation. Each will have its own objectives (enhance market share, defend, introduce products, increase profitability, etc). Smaller businesses will probably only produce one.

3. Market characteristics
This section will look at the current situation within the relevant market and consider the products, competition, brands, characteristics of the market, propensities to buy, types of buyers, trends and the major channels of distribution. It should give readers a good grasp of the key points.

MARKETING PLANNING

WHAT THE PLAN CONTAINS

SUMMARY

OBJECTIVES

MARKET

COMPETITION

4. Competition overview
Details of the competition, its strengths, weaknesses and reactions - so you know what you're up against, and how to differentiate yourself.

5. Product position
This section outlines the strategy for positioning and communicating your products to your customers. It should be stated in terms that your customer understands.

6. Distribution mechanisms
Explains how you will get your products to your customers. What will make the chosen mechanisms effective, what percentage of products will go through each and how it will be measured.

If using agents and associated companies, state how to motivate them and how you can ensure they push your products.

WHAT THE PLAN CONTAINS

7. Selling plan

Includes targets for salesmen, areas and offices; relationships with the distribution network; merchandising materials; sales control and information systems; roles and responsibilities of the sales force; and the billing procedure and accounting mechanism.

8. Communication plan

This section is often sub-divided. It will detail:

- How you will distribute the products
- Pricing and discounting strategies
- Promotional techniques to be used
- The Unique Selling Proposition (USP) you will use to persuade customers to buy your products

9. Timetable

Gives details of timings and should include a time graph (GANTT chart) for ease of understanding.

MARKETING PLANNING

WHAT THE PLAN CONTAINS

10. Responsibilities

A plan is nothing more than a piece of paper if action is not taken to make it happen.

This will set out	**Who**
Must do	**What**
By	**When**

This section also serves as a useful tool for monitoring progress against plan.

11. Budgets

As well as looking at the cost of the intended action, the plan must also consider the financial outcomes of the plan as a whole - ie: the return on expenditure in terms of market share, profit, etc.

An overall budget must, therefore, be prepared to include all costs: direct, indirect and labour. Variance analysis will be conducted against this during the year.

MARKETING PLANNING

PLANNING TIPS

- Start early - time disappears faster than you think
- Involve the right people - they will not buy-in if they have not been consulted
- Discuss it with affected parties prior to finalisation
- Be concise - remember **KISS** (**K**eep **I**t **S**hort & **S**imple)
- Make sure that it supports the overall corporate plan
- Only analyse what is relevant (Pareto's 80:20 Law - 20% of the information will give you 80% of what you want to know)
- Where data is unavailable, either commission research (expensive) or make supportable assumptions
- State any assumptions in the introduction
- Put details in appendices
- Write it with the ultimate reader in mind (Will he understand it?)
- Be realistic
- Get help where you need it
- Make it action-oriented

SUMMARY OBJECTIVES MARKET COMPETITION

TACTICS

TACTICS

OVERVIEW

To put your marketing into action, you have to communicate your offer to your customers - cost effectively and in terms they understand (**address their wants and needs!**).

You need to:

- Use the best and most appropriate communications channels
- Manage your relationship with them
- Get feedback **and act on it**
- Monitor how you are doing against your plan

Essentially, this is the promotional part of the marketing mix.

COMMUNICATIONS CHANNELS

So, what are the main ways of telling customers about your offer?

1 **Advertising**   - press, TV, poster sites, radio
2 **Direct marketing**   - letter, telephone, catalogues
3 **Sales promotion**   - adding an extra offer to make people buy from you
                              and stay with you
4 **Public relations**   - getting media exposure
5 **Promotional
   literature**   - catalogues, brochures, leaflets
6 **Sales force**   - where your people get directly in front of customers
7 **Other channels**   - trade shows, point of sale, merchandising, sponsorship,
                              to name but a few

The challenge is to manage these channels to give the right message, at the right time, within a budget that is always less than that which might be desired!

COMMUNICATIONS CHANNELS

1. ADVERTISING

Advertising puts your message in front of potential (and actual) consumers so that they are disposed to buy from you.

We receive thousands of advertising messages every day - you must make yours stand out. You must decide:

- What message to put
- Where to place the advertisement
- What detail to include
- Which consumers to target

Brand strategy is important and your campaign must support this.

COMMUNICATIONS CHANNELS

1. ADVERTISING

The message

The message will depend on your market research and the impression you want
to create, eg:

- Soap powder adverts focus on technical details - 'our powder washes
  whiter because ...'

- Computer game adverts are oriented towards the young and are often pretty wacky

- Car adverts extol mechanical superiority or lifestyle attributes

- Clothing adverts tell you how to be fashionable and are aspirational

- Software adverts focus on how easy it is to use and the 'functionality' (what it can do)

COMMUNICATIONS CHANNELS

1. ADVERTISING

Where to place the advertisement

Your message will vary according to the medium being used. Media available:

- **TV** - huge audience, animated, colour, sound, expensive
- **Cinema** - smaller audience, very targeted
- **Mainstream press** (eg: the newspapers) - often black and white, no sound, very focused, no movement
- **Specialist press**, (eg: hobby magazines) - often colour, very targeted
- **Posters** - huge impact, difficult to target
- **Radio** - sound, but no vision

Remember the old adage: 'Half your advertising money will be wasted, you just don't know which half!'

COMMUNICATIONS CHANNELS

1. ADVERTISING

What detail to include

The detail depends on the message, the product
and the medium, but you will need to consider:

- Why customers should buy your product
  (aspiration, technical superiority, price, etc);
  benefits first then features

- The price (not always)

- Where to buy it

- How to get in touch

**Remember to feature a memorable
slogan - 'tagline' in the jargon.**

COMMUNICATIONS CHANNELS

1. ADVERTISING

Which consumers to target

This goes back directly to your market segmentation. To decide how and where to place your advert, look at the lifestyles and features of your target markets. Be divergent in your thinking and ask where you find these people. Do they:

- Watch TV?
- Listen to the radio?
- Read a daily paper?
- Read specialist magazines?
- Go to seminars?
- Belong to a trade association?

Use the information from your research to target your communications as well.

COMMUNICATIONS CHANNELS

2. DIRECT MARKETING

Although direct mail often gets a bad press ('junk mail'), it is a very powerful form of customer communication.

- You need a list of potential consumers (possibly with lifestyle or other data attached) with their names, addresses and maybe phone numbers (you can buy these)

- You can also build your own lists (eg: from your own customer data) and cross-sell products

- The content of a mail shot is crucial, as is the response mechanism (should they phone you, clip a coupon or what?); some mail shots are simple personalised letters, others are masterpieces of design

- Think about test mailing to check responses

(Leafleting is really a specialist form of direct mail, except that instead of posting, the literature is placed directly into the letterbox).

COMMUNICATIONS CHANNELS

3. SALES PROMOTION

This can take many forms, and is an incentive for people either to try your product, to start buying from you or buy more. Here are some examples:

- Buy two and get one free
- Collect the coupons and redeem them for £x off the next purchase
- Try our new software free for thirty days
- Enter our exciting new competition
- Join our frequent users' club and benefit from ...

COMMUNICATIONS CHANNELS

4. PUBLIC RELATIONS

Public relations is about creating a favourable image of your company in the minds of stakeholders (public, shareholders, employees, community) to help your products and services. A key mechanism is the use of press releases as well as interviews, syndicated articles, etc. It is considered less biased than advertising.

- Find out what features/surveys a medium is planning and, when relevant to your product/service, provide information.

- Send out news releases when you have something significant to say (a major new contract, a new product, a new Managing Director).

- If a story is newsworthy, if the timing is right (seasonal relevance, within medium's deadline, etc) and if it is relevant and of interest to medium's readers/viewers, then there's a good chance it will be used.

COMMUNICATIONS CHANNELS

5. PROMOTIONAL LITERATURE

- Think carefully: do you need a high quality, glossy corporate brochure, or a set of more specific, functional leaflets?

- Do your customers want technical manuals?

- When they read your literature, how do you want customers to see you? Is it expressed in terms they understand?

- Do you have testimonials from satisfied clients; can you demonstrate the benefits of your product?

- And, above all, when the literature arrives from the printer, how will you distribute it?

COMMUNICATIONS CHANNELS

6. THE SALES FORCE

- Often the most expensive part of your marketing communications, which should be your biggest asset

- Selling is a skilled occupation, so train your sales force well and let it do its job to the best of its ability

- Listen to its requirements and help it

- Supply it with effective, visionary leadership

To most customers the sales force is the human face of your organisation!

(105)

COMMUNICATIONS CHANNELS

7. OTHER CHANNELS

The extent of communications is virtually limitless; here are a few other methods
you might like to consider:

- **Telephone selling** - using trained staff, this can be a cost-effective way of assisting
  your sales force out on the road, making appointments and generating leads

- **Directories and other compendiums** - whilst this is a passive way of marketing,
  many people turn to the Yellow Pages as their first stop in looking for a supplier;
  there are many specialised directories too (like Kompass)

COMMUNICATIONS CHANNELS

7. OTHER CHANNELS

- **Merchandising and point of sale** - when your customer goes into a shop, make sure your goods are attractively displayed

- **Re-sellers or trade intermediaries** - if other people sell your goods on for you, help them in their marketing

- **Sponsorship and product placement** - where appropriate, you can sponsor a good cause or even a TV programme if you feel the association will help your business!

MAKING SURE YOU'RE EFFECTIVE

Here's how to measure the value of each technique.

First, measure the number of calls you get, leads generated and actual sales closed, as well as profit.

- **Advertising** - information is supplied by specialist monitoring organisations; it is called advertising reach

- **Direct mail** - measure the response rate; How many letters were sent, how many replies, leads and sales?

- **Public Relations** - a common method is to work out how many column inches of editorial coverage were generated and then compare this with the cost of actually buying the space; assess the editorial value too

- **Sales force visits** - keep a record of visits and the outcome of these in terms of orders, order size, etc

BEING MARKET-LED
IN PRACTICE

KEY TIPS

This chapter provides key tips to ensure that your organisation is (externally) market-focused, rather than (internally) selling-focused.

- Marketing is not a department - it is an ethos that pervades the whole organisation, so good training and **internal marketing** are crucial

- Always look at issues from the **customer perspective**

- **Keeping customers** is easier than winning new ones (although it may not seem like that when you have a complaint to deal with)

- Prepare a **plan**, follow it and follow it up (**Action not words!**)

- **Get help** where it adds value

- **Remember the CVP!**

INTERNAL MARKETING

- You cannot expect your staff to understand marketing if they have no input into it; all staff from receptionist to MD should be marketing-led

- Keep people informed of new initiatives, products and promotions

- Receptionists, secretaries and telephonists are often the first contacts with your organisation; they have a crucial role to play - don't forget them

- Ask people in the front line for their ideas and customer feedback

- Set up formal training and briefings on marketing issues, and develop your skill base

- Make sure that your marketing meetings include all the disciplines in your firm (production, R&D, packaging, as well as sales and finance, etc)

TAKE CUSTOMER PERSPECTIVE

- Look at things from the customer's viewpoint - he will not see your product with the same glow that you do

- Talk to him and, where appropriate, visit him to see how you can help

- Superficially, all customers want a **better product, delivered yesterday and at a lower price**; but, if talked to sensibly, customers will often tell you just what they do need

- Think of the relationship as a partnership rather than that of host and parasite; get the customer to sell your company as well

- A satisfied customer may well tell you - a dissatisfied customer will definitely tell everybody else!

KEEPING CUSTOMERS

It is more cost-effective to keep customers than to continually win new ones.
Keeping your 'churn rate' (lost customers) as low as possible is a strategic objective.

You must meet their needs!

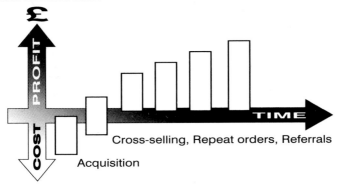

Cross-selling, Repeat orders, Referrals

Acquisition

113

KEEPING CUSTOMERS

Churn rate

This is the rate at which you lose customers and have to replace them just to maintain market share. If your rate is 20%, then potentially every 5 years you have a whole new customer base, each of which costs money to put on the books.

Cross-selling

You can improve the profitability of existing customers significantly by cross-selling other products and services to them. They know you, you have an established relationship, therefore sales costs are lower.

KEEPING CUSTOMERS

DISSATISFACTION CRITERIA

Identify 'at risk' customers by analysing those that you lose. Ask them why they left and then cross-correlate this to their types. This allows you to build up profiles of those likely to leave and the reasons. Consequently, it allows you to let them go or take appropriate action to keep them by changing their dissatisfaction criteria.

Customer type (Socio-Economic)

		AB	C1/2	D/E
Dissatisfaction criteria (why you lose customers)	Price		★	★
	Service level	★	★	
	Delivery time	★	★	

The example above is a very simple criteria analysis for illustration purposes. The star indicates why they might leave and where to focus efforts (service and delivery and an option to re-price).

(115)

KEEPING CUSTOMERS

80:20 RULE

Use the 80:20 rule to get rid of unprofitable customers and keep the profitable ones.

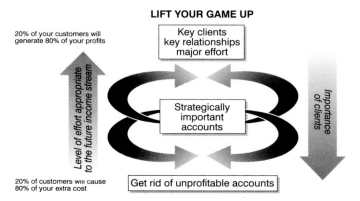

LIFT YOUR GAME UP

20% of your customers will
generate 80% of your profits

Key clients
key relationships
major effort

Strategically
important
accounts

Level of effort appropriate
to the future income stream

Importance
of clients

20% of customers will cause
80% of your extra cost

Get rid of unprofitable accounts

BEING MARKET-LED IN PRACTICE

USING THE PLAN

Marketing costs money. You must ensure cost-effectiveness and focus in your actions.

- Preparing a plan will give direction to your marketing actions and enable you to use valuable, scarce resources to maximise return

- Periodically, review your plan to measure its effectiveness - and revise/flex it as necessary

- Learn lessons from this year for future years

OUTSIDE HELP

It is impossible to be an expert in everything. Even large companies do not have all the resources they require in-house or are not available when needed.

It makes sense to seek help when it is cost-effective to do so or when it is for a non-core skill (You wouldn't service your own gas central heating, would you?).

Experts used by organisations typically include:

- Public relations firms who can place the right messages for you

- Advertising and design agencies for communications that stand out

- Market researchers who can obtain answers faster, more easily and cheaper than you can

- Management consultants who help with analysis, planning, etc

THE CVP

Remember the Customer Value Proposition (CVP):

V isible satisfaction to your customers

A nalyse markets so you understand the dynamics

L ook at your competitors and beat them

U nderstand the real needs of your customers

E qualise value/price equation

BEING MARKET-LED IN PRACTICE

KEY STEPS TO PROFITABLE MARKETING

- Obtain initial customer base
- Keep current/minimise seepage
- Weed out unprofitable ones
- Win new ones
- Where appropriate, cross-sell
- Stick to your CVP

Remember, every customer lost to a firm is one gained by a competitor - be that competitor!

BEING MARKET-LED IN PRACTICE

WHAT IS MARKETING?

M aintain **quality/price** relationship

A lways **listen** to customers

R emember the **need** that you are satisfying

K now your customer

E xplain **benefits** not features

T alk to your customers

I nvolve all staff in marketing

N eeds not wants

G row your market share - profitably

Above all, keep to your CVP

FURTHER READING

'Marketing for Success' by Russell-Jones and Fletcher, Kogan Page

'Value Pricing' by Russell-Jones and Fletcher, Kogan Page

'Principles of Marketing' by Kotler, Prentice Hall

'Marketing Management' by Kotler, Prentice Hall

'Competitive Strategy' by Porter, Free Press

'The Salesperson's Pocketbook' by Clive Bonny, Management Pocketbooks

'The Negotiator's Pocketbook' by Patrick Forsyth, Management Pocketbooks

'The Customer Service Pocketbook' by Tony Newby, Management Pocketbooks

About the Authors

Dr Tony Fletcher is a management consultant and is a member of the Chartered Institute of Marketing. He co-wrote **Marketing for Success** and **Value Pricing** (Kogan Page) with Neil Russell-Jones. He has worked as a marketing manager in both industrial markets and in consumer goods, and as a consultant in over 40 countries. He has given advice, guidance and training on marketing and selling to many organisations in all sectors. He is an advisor for The Prince's Trust, a charity supplying assistance to small inner city businesses in the UK (Patron - HRH The Prince of Wales).

Neil Russell-Jones is a management consultant and is a Chartered Banker, a member of the Strategic Planning Society and an MBA. He has written many articles and several books including **Marketing for Success** and **Value Pricing** (Kogan Page); **The Managing Change Pocketbook** (Management Pocketbooks); and **Financial Services - 1992** (Eurostudy). He has worked with many organisations in the UK, Europe and the USA - particularly in the areas of strategy, BPR, change management, and market entry studies. He is a guest lecturer on the City University Business School's Evening MBA Programme, and has lectured and spoken in many countries to many organisations. He is also an advisor for The Prince's Trust.

All trademarks acknowledged.
© 1996 Tony Fletcher and Neil Russell-Jones

First published in 1996 by Management Pocketbooks Ltd
14 East Street, Alresford, Hampshire SO24 9EE

Printed in England by Alresford Press Ltd
Prospect Road, Alresford, Hants SO24 9QF

ISBN 1870471 40 7

ORDER FORM

Your details

Name _____

Position _____

Company _____

Address _____

_____

_____

_____

Telephone _____

Facsimile _____

VAT No. (EC companies) _____

Your Order Ref _____

Please send me:

No. copies

The _____Marketing_____ Pocketbook ☐

The _____ Pocketbook ☐

The _____ Pocketbook ☐

The _____ Pocketbook ☐

The _____ Pocketbook ☐

The _____ Pocketbook ☐

The _____ Pocketbook ☐

MANAGEMENT POCKETBOOKS

14 EAST STREET ALRESFORD
HAMPSHIRE SO24 9EE
Tel: (01962) 735573
Fax: (01962) 733637

THE MANAGEMENT POCKETBOOK SERIES

The Appraisals Pocketbook
The Balance Sheet Pocketbook
The Business Presenter's Pocketbook
The Business Writing Pocketbook
Challengers!
The Communicator's Pocketbook
The Creative Manager's Pocketbook
The Cultural Gaffes Pocketbook
The Customer Service Pocketbook
The Export Pocketbook
The Interviewer's Pocketbook
The Key Accounts Manager Pocketbook
The Learner's Pocketbook
The Managing Budgets Pocketbook
The Managing Cashflow Pocketbook
The Managing Change Pocketbook
The Managing Your Appraisal Pocketbook
The Manager's Pocketbook

The Manager's Training Pocketbook
The Marketing Pocketbook
The Meetings Pocketbook
The Negotiator's Pocketbook
The People Manager's Pocketbook
The Quality Pocketbook
The Salesperson's Pocketbook
The Team Builder's Pocketfile of
Ready-to-copy Exercises
The Teamworking Pocketbook
The Telesales Pocketbook
The Time Management Pocketbook
Tips for Presenters audio cassette
Tips for Trainers audio cassette
The Trainer Standards Pocketbook
The Trainer's Pocketbook
The Trainer's Pocketbook of
Ready-to-use Exercises

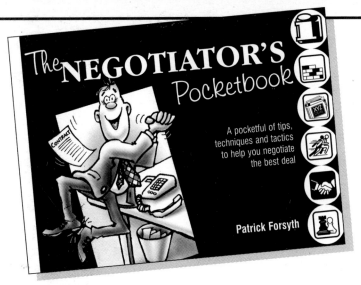

Other titles in the Pocketbook series include: **The Salesperson's Pocketbook,**
The Export Pocketbook, The Customer Service Pocketbook, The Telesales
Pocketbook and (illustrated) **The Negotiator's Pocketbook.**